THIS JOURNAL BELONGS TO

DATE:_____ DAY:_____

TODAY'S VERSE

LORD TEACH ME TO

I AM THANKFUL FOR

PRAYER REQUESTS

DATE:_____ DAY:_____

TODAY'S VERSE

LORD TEACH ME TO

I AM THANKFUL FOR

PRAYER REQUESTS

DATE:_____ DAY:_____

TODAY'S VERSE

LORD TEACH ME TO

I AM THANKFUL FOR

PRAYER REQUESTS

DATE:_____ DAY:_____

TODAY'S VERSE

LORD TEACH ME TO

I AM THANKFUL FOR

PRAYER REQUESTS

DATE:_____ DAY:_____

TODAY'S VERSE

LORD TEACH ME TO

I AM THANKFUL FOR

PRAYER REQUESTS

DATE:_____ DAY:_____

TODAY'S VERSE

LORD TEACH ME TO

I AM THANKFUL FOR

PRAYER REQUESTS

DATE:_____ DAY:_____

TODAY'S VERSE

LORD TEACH ME TO

I AM THANKFUL FOR

PRAYER REQUESTS

DATE:_____ DAY:_____

TODAY'S VERSE

LORD TEACH ME TO

I AM THANKFUL FOR

PRAYER REQUESTS

DATE:_____ DAY:_____

TODAY'S VERSE

LORD TEACH ME TO

I AM THANKFUL FOR

PRAYER REQUESTS

DATE:_____ DAY:_____

TODAY'S VERSE

LORD TEACH ME TO

_____
_____
_____
_____
_____
_____
_____
_____
_____
_____
_____
_____
_____
_____
_____

I AM THANKFUL FOR

_____
_____
_____
_____
_____
_____
_____
_____
_____
_____
_____

PRAYER REQUESTS

DATE:_____ DAY:_____

TODAY'S VERSE

LORD TEACH ME TO

I AM THANKFUL FOR

PRAYER REQUESTS

TODAY'S VERSE

LORD TEACH ME TO

I AM THANKFUL FOR

PRAYER REQUESTS

DATE:_____ DAY:_____

TODAY'S VERSE

LORD TEACH ME TO

I AM THANKFUL FOR

PRAYER REQUESTS

DATE:_____ DAY:_____

TODAY'S VERSE

LORD TEACH ME TO

I AM THANKFUL FOR

PRAYER REQUESTS

DATE:_____ DAY:_____

TODAY'S VERSE

LORD TEACH ME TO

I AM THANKFUL FOR

PRAYER REQUESTS

DATE:_____ DAY:_____

TODAY'S VERSE

LORD TEACH ME TO

I AM THANKFUL FOR

PRAYER REQUESTS

DATE:_____ DAY:_____

TODAY'S VERSE

LORD TEACH ME TO

I AM THANKFUL FOR

PRAYER REQUESTS

DATE:_____ DAY:_____

TODAY'S VERSE

LORD TEACH ME TO

_____
_____
_____
_____
_____
_____
_____
_____
_____
_____
_____
_____

I AM THANKFUL FOR

_____
_____
_____
_____
_____
_____
_____
_____
_____
_____
_____
_____
_____
_____

PRAYER REQUESTS

DATE:_____ DAY:_____

TODAY'S VERSE

LORD TEACH ME TO	I AM THANKFUL FOR

PRAYER REQUESTS

DATE:_____ DAY:_____

TODAY'S VERSE

LORD TEACH ME TO

I AM THANKFUL FOR

PRAYER REQUESTS

DATE:_____ DAY:_____

TODAY'S VERSE

LORD TEACH ME TO

I AM THANKFUL FOR

PRAYER REQUESTS

DATE:_____ DAY:_____

TODAY'S VERSE

LORD TEACH ME TO

I AM THANKFUL FOR

PRAYER REQUESTS

TODAY'S VERSE

LORD TEACH ME TO

I AM THANKFUL FOR

PRAYER REQUESTS

DATE:_____ DAY:_____

TODAY'S VERSE

LORD TEACH ME TO

I AM THANKFUL FOR

PRAYER REQUESTS

DATE:_____ DAY:_____

TODAY'S VERSE

LORD TEACH ME TO

I AM THANKFUL FOR

PRAYER REQUESTS

DATE:_____ DAY:_____

TODAY'S VERSE

LORD TEACH ME TO

I AM THANKFUL FOR

PRAYER REQUESTS

DATE:_____ DAY:_____

TODAY'S VERSE

LORD TEACH ME TO	I AM THANKFUL FOR

PRAYER REQUESTS

DATE:_____ DAY:_____

TODAY'S VERSE

LORD TEACH ME TO

I AM THANKFUL FOR

PRAYER REQUESTS

TODAY'S VERSE

LORD TEACH ME TO

I AM THANKFUL FOR

PRAYER REQUESTS

DATE:_____ DAY:_____

TODAY'S VERSE

LORD TEACH ME TO

I AM THANKFUL FOR

PRAYER REQUESTS

DATE:_____ DAY:_____

TODAY'S VERSE

LORD TEACH ME TO

_____
_____
_____
_____
_____
_____
_____
_____
_____
_____
_____
_____
_____
_____

I AM THANKFUL FOR

_____
_____
_____
_____
_____
_____
_____
_____
_____
_____
_____
_____

PRAYER REQUESTS

DATE:_____ DAY:_____

TODAY'S VERSE

LORD TEACH ME TO

I AM THANKFUL FOR

PRAYER REQUESTS

DATE:_____ DAY:_____

TODAY'S VERSE

LORD TEACH ME TO

_____
_____
_____
_____
_____
_____
_____
_____
_____
_____
_____
_____
_____
_____
_____

I AM THANKFUL FOR

_____
_____
_____
_____
_____
_____
_____
_____
_____
_____
_____
_____
_____

PRAYER REQUESTS

DATE:_____ DAY:_____

TODAY'S VERSE

LORD TEACH ME TO

I AM THANKFUL FOR

PRAYER REQUESTS

DATE:_____ DAY:_____

TODAY'S VERSE

LORD TEACH ME TO

I AM THANKFUL FOR

PRAYER REQUESTS

DATE:_____ DAY:_____

TODAY'S VERSE

LORD TEACH ME TO

I AM THANKFUL FOR

PRAYER REQUESTS

DATE:_____ DAY:_____

TODAY'S VERSE

LORD TEACH ME TO

I AM THANKFUL FOR

PRAYER REQUESTS

DATE:_____ DAY:_____

TODAY'S VERSE

LORD TEACH ME TO

_____
_____
_____
_____
_____
_____
_____
_____
_____
_____
_____
_____
_____
_____
_____
_____

I AM THANKFUL FOR

_____
_____
_____
_____
_____
_____
_____
_____
_____
_____
_____
_____
_____
_____
_____
_____
_____

PRAYER REQUESTS

DATE:_____ DAY:_____

TODAY'S VERSE

LORD TEACH ME TO

I AM THANKFUL FOR

PRAYER REQUESTS

DATE:_____ DAY:_____

TODAY'S VERSE

LORD TEACH ME TO

I AM THANKFUL FOR

PRAYER REQUESTS

DATE:_____ DAY:_____

TODAY'S VERSE

LORD TEACH ME TO

I AM THANKFUL FOR

PRAYER REQUESTS

DATE:_____ DAY:_____

TODAY'S VERSE

LORD TEACH ME TO	I AM THANKFUL FOR

PRAYER REQUESTS

DATE:_____ DAY:_____

TODAY'S VERSE

LORD TEACH ME TO

I AM THANKFUL FOR

PRAYER REQUESTS

DATE:_____ DAY:_____

TODAY'S VERSE

LORD TEACH ME TO

I AM THANKFUL FOR

PRAYER REQUESTS

DATE:_____ DAY:_____

TODAY'S VERSE

LORD TEACH ME TO

I AM THANKFUL FOR

PRAYER REQUESTS

DATE:_____ DAY:_____

TODAY'S VERSE

LORD TEACH ME TO

I AM THANKFUL FOR

PRAYER REQUESTS

DATE:_____ DAY:_____

TODAY'S VERSE

LORD TEACH ME TO

I AM THANKFUL FOR

PRAYER REQUESTS

DATE:_____ DAY:_____

TODAY'S VERSE

LORD TEACH ME TO

I AM THANKFUL FOR

PRAYER REQUESTS

DATE:_____ DAY:_____

TODAY'S VERSE

LORD TEACH ME TO

I AM THANKFUL FOR

PRAYER REQUESTS

DATE:_____ DAY:_____

TODAY'S VERSE

LORD TEACH ME TO

I AM THANKFUL FOR

PRAYER REQUESTS

DATE:_____ DAY:_____

TODAY'S VERSE

LORD TEACH ME TO

_____
_____
_____
_____
_____
_____
_____
_____
_____
_____
_____
_____
_____
_____
_____

I AM THANKFUL FOR

_____
_____
_____
_____
_____
_____
_____
_____
_____
_____
_____
_____

PRAYER REQUESTS

DATE:_____ DAY:_____

TODAY'S VERSE

LORD TEACH ME TO

I AM THANKFUL FOR

PRAYER REQUESTS

DATE:_____ DAY:_____

TODAY'S VERSE

LORD TEACH ME TO

_____
_____
_____
_____
_____
_____
_____
_____
_____
_____
_____
_____
_____
_____
_____
_____

I AM THANKFUL FOR

_____
_____
_____
_____
_____
_____
_____
_____
_____
_____
_____
_____
_____
_____
_____

PRAYER REQUESTS

DATE:_____ DAY:_____

TODAY'S VERSE

LORD TEACH ME TO

I AM THANKFUL FOR

PRAYER REQUESTS

DATE:_____ DAY:_____

TODAY'S VERSE

LORD TEACH ME TO

I AM THANKFUL FOR

PRAYER REQUESTS

DATE:_____ DAY:_____

TODAY'S VERSE

LORD TEACH ME TO

I AM THANKFUL FOR

PRAYER REQUESTS

DATE:_____ DAY:_____

TODAY'S VERSE

LORD TEACH ME TO

I AM THANKFUL FOR

PRAYER REQUESTS

DATE:_____ DAY:_____

TODAY'S VERSE

LORD TEACH ME TO

I AM THANKFUL FOR

PRAYER REQUESTS

DATE:_____ DAY:_____

TODAY'S VERSE

LORD TEACH ME TO

I AM THANKFUL FOR

PRAYER REQUESTS

DATE:_____ DAY:_____

TODAY'S VERSE

LORD TEACH ME TO

I AM THANKFUL FOR

PRAYER REQUESTS

DATE:_____ DAY:_____

TODAY'S VERSE

LORD TEACH ME TO

I AM THANKFUL FOR

PRAYER REQUESTS

DATE:_____ DAY:_____

TODAY'S VERSE

LORD TEACH ME TO

I AM THANKFUL FOR

PRAYER REQUESTS

DATE:_____ DAY:_____

TODAY'S VERSE

LORD TEACH ME TO

_____
_____
_____
_____
_____
_____
_____
_____
_____
_____
_____
_____
_____
_____
_____
_____

I AM THANKFUL FOR

_____
_____
_____
_____
_____
_____
_____
_____
_____
_____
_____
_____
_____
_____
_____

PRAYER REQUESTS

DATE:_____ DAY:_____

TODAY'S VERSE

LORD TEACH ME TO	I AM THANKFUL FOR

PRAYER REQUESTS

DATE:_____ DAY:_____

TODAY'S VERSE

LORD TEACH ME TO

I AM THANKFUL FOR

PRAYER REQUESTS

DATE:_____ DAY:_____

TODAY'S VERSE

LORD TEACH ME TO

_____
_____
_____
_____
_____
_____
_____
_____
_____
_____
_____
_____
_____
_____
_____

I AM THANKFUL FOR

_____
_____
_____
_____
_____
_____
_____
_____
_____
_____
_____
_____
_____
_____

PRAYER REQUESTS

DATE:_____ DAY:_____

TODAY'S VERSE

LORD TEACH ME TO

I AM THANKFUL FOR

PRAYER REQUESTS

DATE:_____ DAY:_____

TODAY'S VERSE

LORD TEACH ME TO

I AM THANKFUL FOR

PRAYER REQUESTS

DATE:_____ DAY:_____

TODAY'S VERSE

LORD TEACH ME TO

I AM THANKFUL FOR

PRAYER REQUESTS

DATE:_____ DAY:_____

TODAY'S VERSE

LORD TEACH ME TO

I AM THANKFUL FOR

PRAYER REQUESTS

DATE:_____ DAY:_____

TODAY'S VERSE

LORD TEACH ME TO

I AM THANKFUL FOR

PRAYER REQUESTS

DATE:_____ DAY:_____

TODAY'S VERSE

LORD TEACH ME TO

I AM THANKFUL FOR

PRAYER REQUESTS

DATE:_____ DAY:_____

TODAY'S VERSE

LORD TEACH ME TO

I AM THANKFUL FOR

PRAYER REQUESTS

DATE:_____ DAY:_____

TODAY'S VERSE

LORD TEACH ME TO

I AM THANKFUL FOR

PRAYER REQUESTS

DATE:_____ DAY:_____

TODAY'S VERSE

LORD TEACH ME TO

I AM THANKFUL FOR

PRAYER REQUESTS

DATE:_____ DAY:_____

TODAY'S VERSE

LORD TEACH ME TO

I AM THANKFUL FOR

PRAYER REQUESTS

DATE:_____ DAY:_____

TODAY'S VERSE

LORD TEACH ME TO

I AM THANKFUL FOR

PRAYER REQUESTS

DATE:_____ DAY:_____

TODAY'S VERSE

LORD TEACH ME TO

I AM THANKFUL FOR

PRAYER REQUESTS

DATE:_____ DAY:_____

TODAY'S VERSE

LORD TEACH ME TO

_____
_____
_____
_____
_____
_____
_____
_____
_____
_____
_____
_____
_____
_____

I AM THANKFUL FOR

_____
_____
_____
_____
_____
_____
_____
_____
_____
_____
_____

PRAYER REQUESTS

DATE:_____ DAY:_____

TODAY'S VERSE

LORD TEACH ME TO

I AM THANKFUL FOR

PRAYER REQUESTS

DATE:_____ DAY:_____

TODAY'S VERSE

LORD TEACH ME TO

I AM THANKFUL FOR

PRAYER REQUESTS

TODAY'S VERSE

LORD TEACH ME TO

I AM THANKFUL FOR

PRAYER REQUESTS

DATE:_____ DAY:_____

TODAY'S VERSE

LORD TEACH ME TO

I AM THANKFUL FOR

PRAYER REQUESTS

DATE:_____ DAY:_____

TODAY'S VERSE

LORD TEACH ME TO

I AM THANKFUL FOR

PRAYER REQUESTS

DATE:_____ DAY:_____

TODAY'S VERSE

LORD TEACH ME TO

I AM THANKFUL FOR

PRAYER REQUESTS

DATE:_____ DAY:_____

TODAY'S VERSE

LORD TEACH ME TO

_____
_____
_____
_____
_____
_____
_____
_____
_____
_____
_____
_____
_____
_____

I AM THANKFUL FOR

_____
_____
_____
_____
_____
_____
_____
_____
_____
_____
_____
_____
_____

PRAYER REQUESTS

DATE:_____ DAY:_____

TODAY'S VERSE

LORD TEACH ME TO

I AM THANKFUL FOR

PRAYER REQUESTS

DATE:_____ DAY:_____

TODAY'S VERSE

LORD TEACH ME TO

I AM THANKFUL FOR

PRAYER REQUESTS

DATE:_____ DAY:_____

TODAY'S VERSE

LORD TEACH ME TO

I AM THANKFUL FOR

PRAYER REQUESTS

DATE:_____ DAY:_____

TODAY'S VERSE

LORD TEACH ME TO

I AM THANKFUL FOR

PRAYER REQUESTS

DATE:_____ DAY:_____

TODAY'S VERSE

LORD TEACH ME TO

I AM THANKFUL FOR

PRAYER REQUESTS

DATE:_____ DAY:_____

TODAY'S VERSE

LORD TEACH ME TO

I AM THANKFUL FOR

PRAYER REQUESTS

DATE:_____ DAY:_____

TODAY'S VERSE

LORD TEACH ME TO

_____
_____
_____
_____
_____
_____
_____
_____
_____
_____
_____
_____
_____
_____
_____

I AM THANKFUL FOR

_____
_____
_____
_____
_____
_____
_____
_____
_____
_____
_____
_____

PRAYER REQUESTS

DATE:_____ DAY:_____

TODAY'S VERSE

LORD TEACH ME TO

I AM THANKFUL FOR

PRAYER REQUESTS

DATE:_____ DAY:_____

TODAY'S VERSE

LORD TEACH ME TO

I AM THANKFUL FOR

PRAYER REQUESTS

DATE:_____ DAY:_____

TODAY'S VERSE

LORD TEACH ME TO

I AM THANKFUL FOR

PRAYER REQUESTS

DATE:_____ DAY:_____

TODAY'S VERSE

LORD TEACH ME TO

I AM THANKFUL FOR

PRAYER REQUESTS

DATE:_____ DAY:_____

TODAY'S VERSE

LORD TEACH ME TO

I AM THANKFUL FOR

PRAYER REQUESTS

DATE:_____ DAY:_____

TODAY'S VERSE

LORD TEACH ME TO

I AM THANKFUL FOR

PRAYER REQUESTS

DATE:_____ DAY:_____

TODAY'S VERSE

LORD TEACH ME TO

I AM THANKFUL FOR

PRAYER REQUESTS

TODAY'S VERSE

LORD TEACH ME TO

I AM THANKFUL FOR

PRAYER REQUESTS

DATE:_____ DAY:_____

TODAY'S VERSE

LORD TEACH ME TO

I AM THANKFUL FOR

PRAYER REQUESTS

DATE:_____ DAY:_____

TODAY'S VERSE

LORD TEACH ME TO

_____
_____
_____
_____
_____
_____
_____
_____
_____
_____
_____
_____
_____
_____

I AM THANKFUL FOR

_____
_____
_____
_____
_____
_____
_____
_____
_____
_____
_____
_____
_____
_____

PRAYER REQUESTS

DATE:_____ DAY:_____

TODAY'S VERSE

LORD TEACH ME TO

I AM THANKFUL FOR

PRAYER REQUESTS

DATE:_____ DAY:_____

TODAY'S VERSE

LORD TEACH ME TO

I AM THANKFUL FOR

PRAYER REQUESTS

DATE:_____ DAY:_____

TODAY'S VERSE

LORD TEACH ME TO

I AM THANKFUL FOR

PRAYER REQUESTS

DATE:_____ DAY:_____

TODAY'S VERSE

LORD TEACH ME TO

I AM THANKFUL FOR

PRAYER REQUESTS

DATE:_____ DAY:_____

TODAY'S VERSE

LORD TEACH ME TO

I AM THANKFUL FOR

PRAYER REQUESTS

TODAY'S VERSE

LORD TEACH ME TO

I AM THANKFUL FOR

PRAYER REQUESTS

DATE:_____ DAY:_____

TODAY'S VERSE

LORD TEACH ME TO

I AM THANKFUL FOR

PRAYER REQUESTS

DATE:_____ DAY:_____

TODAY'S VERSE

LORD TEACH ME TO

I AM THANKFUL FOR

PRAYER REQUESTS

DATE:_____ DAY:_____

TODAY'S VERSE

LORD TEACH ME TO

I AM THANKFUL FOR

PRAYER REQUESTS

DATE:_____ DAY:_____

TODAY'S VERSE

LORD TEACH ME TO

I AM THANKFUL FOR

PRAYER REQUESTS

DATE:_____ DAY:_____

TODAY'S VERSE

LORD TEACH ME TO

I AM THANKFUL FOR

PRAYER REQUESTS

DATE:_____ DAY:_____

TODAY'S VERSE

LORD TEACH ME TO

I AM THANKFUL FOR

PRAYER REQUESTS

DATE:_____ DAY:_____

TODAY'S VERSE

LORD TEACH ME TO

I AM THANKFUL FOR

PRAYER REQUESTS

DATE:_____ DAY:_____

TODAY'S VERSE

LORD TEACH ME TO

I AM THANKFUL FOR

PRAYER REQUESTS

DATE:_____ DAY:_____

TODAY'S VERSE

LORD TEACH ME TO

I AM THANKFUL FOR

PRAYER REQUESTS

DATE:_____ DAY:_____

TODAY'S VERSE

LORD TEACH ME TO

I AM THANKFUL FOR

PRAYER REQUESTS

DATE:_____ DAY:_____

TODAY'S VERSE

LORD TEACH ME TO

I AM THANKFUL FOR

PRAYER REQUESTS

DATE:_____ DAY:_____

TODAY'S VERSE

LORD TEACH ME TO

I AM THANKFUL FOR

PRAYER REQUESTS

DATE:_____ DAY:_____

TODAY'S VERSE

LORD TEACH ME TO

I AM THANKFUL FOR

PRAYER REQUESTS

DATE:_____ DAY:_____

TODAY'S VERSE

LORD TEACH ME TO

I AM THANKFUL FOR

PRAYER REQUESTS

DATE:_____ DAY:_____

TODAY'S VERSE

LORD TEACH ME TO

I AM THANKFUL FOR

PRAYER REQUESTS

Made in the USA
Coppell, TX
23 October 2021